MW01107783

SECRETS OF THE ANIMAL WORLD

WHALES
Giant Marine Mammals

by Andreu Llamas
Illustrated by Gabriel Casadevall and Ali Garousi

Gareth Stevens Publishing
MILWAUKEE

For a free color catalog describing Gareth Stevens' list of high-quality books, call 1-800-542-2595 (USA) or 1-800-461-9120 (Canada). Gareth Stevens' Fax: (414) 225-0377.

The editor would like to extend special thanks to Jan W. Rafert, Curator of Primates and Small Mammals, Milwaukee County Zoo, Milwaukee, Wisconsin, for his kind and professional help with the information in this book.

Library of Congress Cataloging-in-Publication Data

Llamas, Andreu.
    [Ballena. English]
    Whales: giant marine mammals / by Andreu Llamas; illustrated by Gabriel Casadevall and Ali Garousi.
        p. cm. — (Secrets of the animal world)
    Includes bibliographical references (p.) and index.
    Filmography: p.
    Summary: provides detailed descriptions of the physical characteristics and behavior of whales.
    ISBN 0-8368-1398-7 (lib. bdg.)
    1. Whales—Juvenile literature. [1. Whales.] I. Casadevall, Gabriel, ill. II. Garousi, Ali, ill. III. Title. IV. Series.
QL737.C4L5813 1996
599.5—dc20   95-45800

This edition first published in 1996 by
Gareth Stevens Publishing
1555 North RiverCenter Drive, Suite 201
Milwaukee, Wisconsin 53212 USA

This edition © 1996 by Gareth Stevens, Inc. Created with original © 1993 Ediciones Este, S.A., Barcelona, Spain. Additional end matter © 1996 by Gareth Stevens, Inc.

Series editor: Patricia Lantier-Sampon
Editorial assistants: Diane Laska, Rita Reitci, Derek Smith

Printed in the United States of America

1 2 3 4 5 6 7 8 9 99 98 97 96

CONTENTS

THE WORLD OF WHALES

Where whales live

Whales are the largest mammals that have ever existed on Earth, and they live in the oceans and seas. These gigantic animals can measure up to 100 feet (30 meters) in length and weigh over 165 tons (150 metric tons).

Whales live in all the world's oceans, and they thrive in such varied environments as temperate and tropical waters, as well as the arctic seas near the North and South poles. They can live in both the high seas and coastal waters.

Deep ocean waters support the weight of the enormous whales.

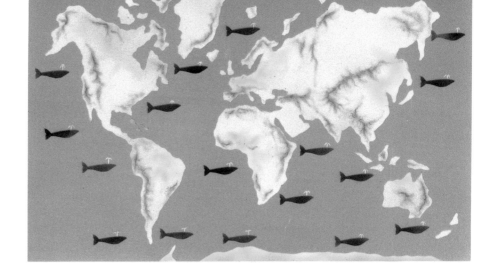

Whales live in the oceans that cover three-quarters of Earth's surface.

Mammals like ourselves

Although they live in the ocean, whales are not fishes. In fact, they are mammals like ourselves. This means whales breathe air into their lungs, and their body is covered in skin. They are also warm-blooded; their body temperature remains more or less stable at 98.6°F (37°C). The water temperature below the surface of the sea can be near-freezing, and heat loss through the skin is greater under the water than in the air. To avoid feeling cold, whales have a layer of fat, or blubber, up to 20 inches (50 cm) thick under their skin that keeps out the cold.

Whales play with objects by sinking and tossing them.

Types of whales

Whales belong to the order Cetacea, which includes animals that live in the sea. Cetaceans are divided into three suborders: Archaeoceti — a group of toothed whales that are now extinct; Odontoceti — toothed whales, as well as dolphins and porpoises; and Mysticeti — baleen, or whalebone, whales that do not have teeth. There are seventy-six known species of Cetaceans.

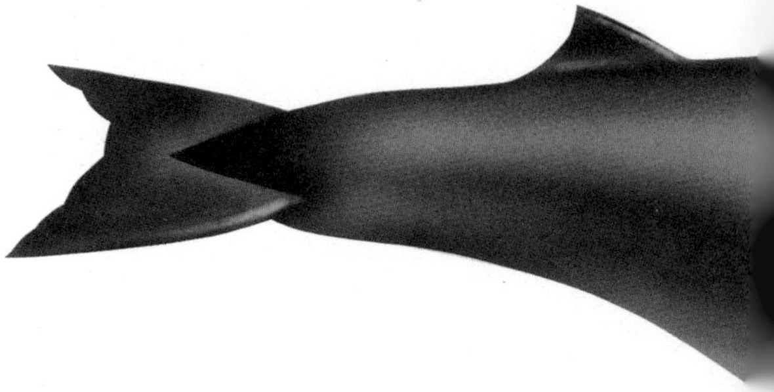

PYGMY RIGHT WHALE

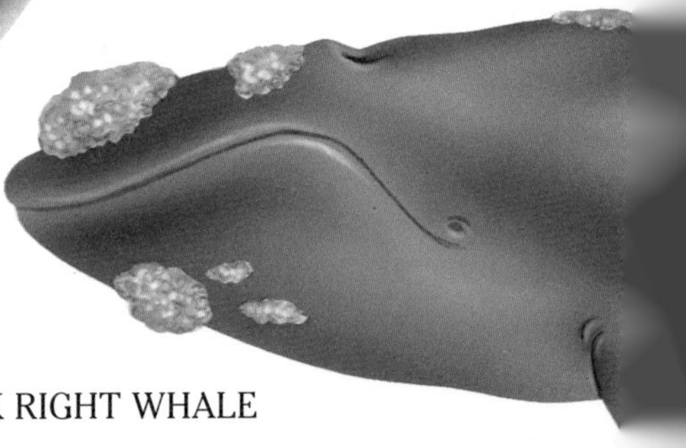

BLACK RIGHT WHALE

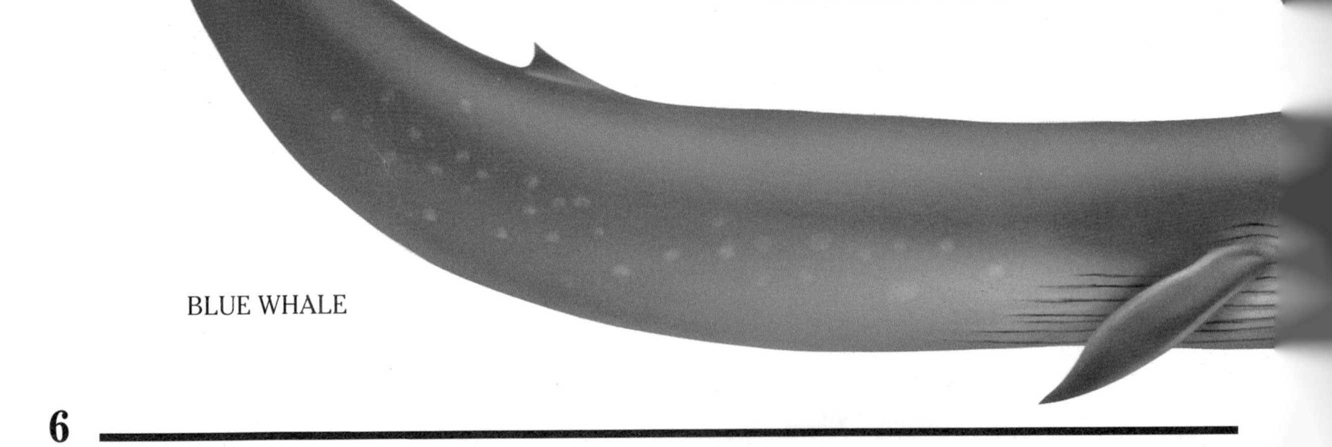

BLUE WHALE

6

FIN WHALE

HUMPBACK WHALE

GRAY WHALE

There are three baleen whale families. The first family includes rorqual whales, such as the blue whale — the largest animal ever to inhabit Earth. The second family includes right whales, with three species that can measure up to 60 feet (18 m) long. This family also includes the pygmy right whale, which measures "only" 20 feet (6 m) in length and weighs 5 tons (4.5 metric tons). The third family includes the gray whale, which measures up to 50 feet (15 m) in length.

INSIDE THE WHALE

A whale's body is well adapted for life in the water. Water resistance caused by the friction between skin and water slows the animal's movement. To reduce this friction, the whale's body has a hydrodynamic shape; it is smooth and tapered at the ends, which helps it move swiftly. Here you can see some of the characteristics that help whales survive their watery environment.

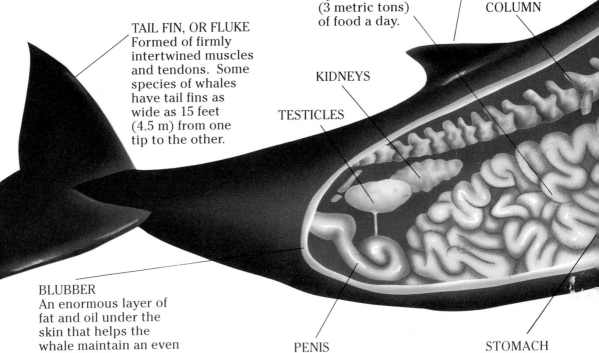

BLOWHOLE
A series of ducts and valves that can open and close to stop water from entering the whale's nostrils.

DORSAL FIN
Most whales have a dorsal fin on the middle of their back or slightly farther back. This fin does not have bones. Instead, it is lined with a fibrous tissue.

INTESTINE
Varies in length according to the species; enables the whale to digest up to 3.3 tons (3 metric tons) of food a day.

VERTEBRAL COLUMN

TAIL FIN, OR FLUKE
Formed of firmly intertwined muscles and tendons. Some species of whales have tail fins as wide as 15 feet (4.5 m) from one tip to the other.

KIDNEYS

TESTICLES

BLUBBER
An enormous layer of fat and oil under the skin that helps the whale maintain an even body temperature.

PENIS

STOMACH

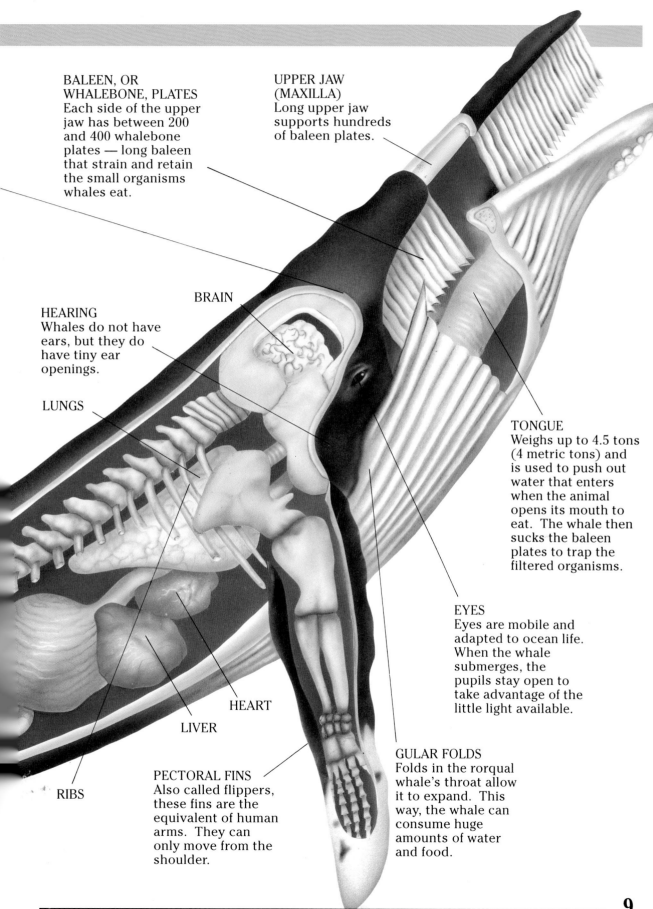

BALEEN, OR
WHALEBONE, PLATES
Each side of the upper
jaw has between 200
and 400 whalebone
plates — long baleen
that strain and retain
the small organisms
whales eat.

UPPER JAW
(MAXILLA)
Long upper jaw
supports hundreds
of baleen plates.

BRAIN

HEARING
Whales do not have
ears, but they do
have tiny ear
openings.

LUNGS

TONGUE
Weighs up to 4.5 tons
(4 metric tons) and
is used to push out
water that enters
when the animal
opens its mouth to
eat. The whale then
sucks the baleen
plates to trap the
filtered organisms.

EYES
Eyes are mobile and
adapted to ocean life.
When the whale
submerges, the
pupils stay open to
take advantage of the
little light available.

HEART

LIVER

PECTORAL FINS
Also called flippers,
these fins are the
equivalent of human
arms. They can
only move from the
shoulder.

GULAR FOLDS
Folds in the rorqual
whale's throat allow
it to expand. This
way, the whale can
consume huge
amounts of water
and food.

RIBS

9

THE LARGEST CREATURES IN THE WORLD

Growing and growing

Large animals are not always fierce. Generally, the larger the animal, the calmer its character.

A large body reduces an animal's heat loss in water. As the animal grows, its volume increases much more than its body surface. As a result, a large animal such as the whale has a proportionally smaller surface area in contact with cold water than a smaller animal. This is a great advantage for whales, especially in the icy waters of the polar regions.

It must be thrilling for a diver to swim alongside an enormous whale that weighs two thousand times more than she or he does.

In spite of its size, the whale is not very aggressive. Scientists often approach whales without being attacked.

that killer whales attack other whales?

Adult whales have few enemies. Only killer whales traveling in groups dare to attack larger whales. Spectacular chases take place in which the killer whales bite their victims to weaken and drown them.

A group, or pod, of killer whales is very organized when attacking. One throws itself onto the head of its victim to block its blowhole and suffocate it. When the whale becomes exhausted, the pod devours it.

Growth of a giant

Any increase in body size for mammals living on dry land makes the animal slower because of gravity. But gravity does not affect the ocean-dwelling whale's enormous size because the water supports much of its weight.

The unborn young whale develops from five hundred to one thousand times faster than an unborn human. During the last months of gestation, the blue whale calf gains more than 2.2 tons (2 metric tons), and during the last days before being born, it gains as much as 220 pounds (100 kg) a day.

The female whale, called the cow, produces milk that is rich in fat and proteins, which the calves need to grow rapidly. The blue whale calf gains about

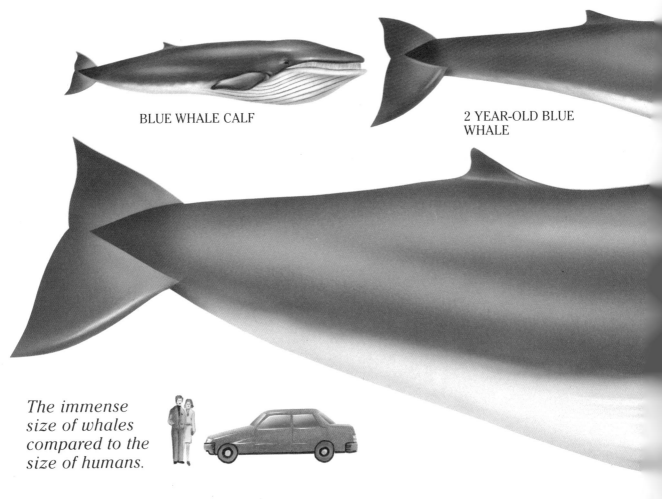

BLUE WHALE CALF

2 YEAR-OLD BLUE WHALE

The immense size of whales compared to the size of humans.

190 pounds (86 kg) a day, for a total of about 20 tons (18 metric tons) during the seven-month lactation period! During this time, it consumes about 40 gallons (150 liters) of milk a day. The blue whale calf, which is 26 feet (8 m) long and weighs 7.7 tons (7 metric tons) at birth, will reach a length of 52 feet (16 m) when two years old. By adulthood, the blue whale is 115 feet (35 m) in length and can weigh up to165 tons (150 metric tons).

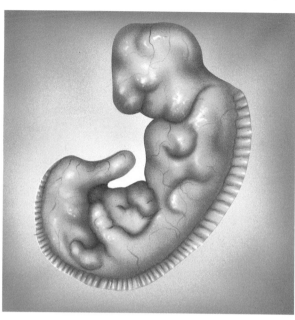

The blue whale young gains more than 2.2 tons (2 metric tons) during the last two months of gestation.

FULLY GROWN ADULT
BLUE WHALE

FOOD FOR GIANTS

Filters instead of teeth

Whales and Mysticeti in general feed by filtering the water with their baleen, or whalebone, plates. These elastic, hornlike plates are located on the upper jaw. They filter out plankton for the whale to eat. The baleen plates are long, measuring from 3 to 15 feet (1 to 4.5 m), and are made of a material similar to human fingernails. The number of baleen plates a whale has depends on the species; it varies from two hundred to four thousand on each side of the

From close up, the baleen looks like a series of parallel elastic plates.

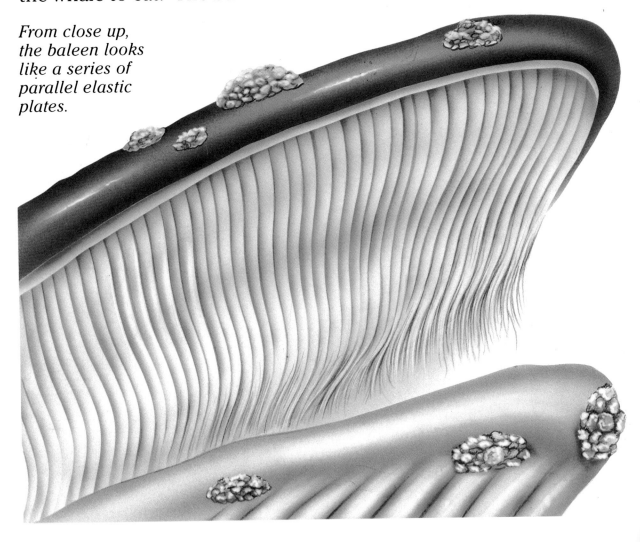

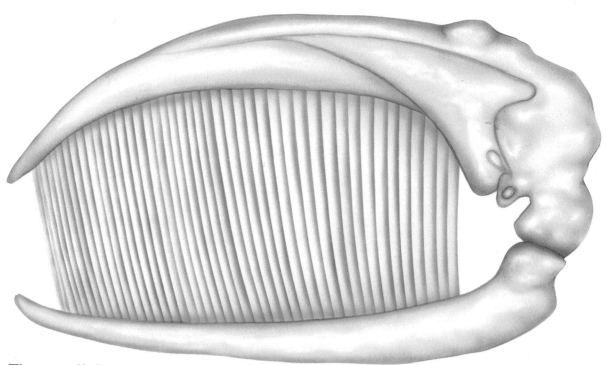

*The parallel
baleen plates
are 0.2-0.3 inches
(6-7 mm) apart.*

*These horny
plates are taller
than an adult
human.*

upper jaw. When the whale
opens its mouth, enormous
amounts of water containing
plankton flood in. Its tongue,
which is attached to the jaw
instead of hanging free at the
end, moves like a piston and
expels the water. The food
retained in its baleen goes down
the animal's esophagus and into
its huge stomach, which is
divided into various chambers.

that whales sing?

Sailors and fishermen can sometimes hear the mysterious and melodic songs of the whales. These "songs" are made up of a sequence of different sounds that can last for ten minutes or more and are then repeated over and over again in exactly the same order. The songs vary according to the species of whale. Below, you can see the *S*-shaped position the whale adopts when it sings.

Small food for giants

The whale's diet consists mainly of krill, an assortment of small crustaceans that live in huge quantities in the upper layers of the coldest seas. Krill reproduces at about 110 million tons (100 million metric tons) a year. Whales need at least 3.3 to 4.4 tons (3 to 4 metric tons) of krill a day. Since krill is so tiny, whales have to swallow enormous amounts of water to collect enough food. The whale stomach is adapted to this diet; for instance, rorqual whales can take in up to one ton of krill in their first stomachs.

The tiny, abundant crustaceans that form krill each measure about 0.4 inches (10 mm) long.

A rorqual whale has about fifty gular folds in its throat that can expand to take in huge amounts of water.

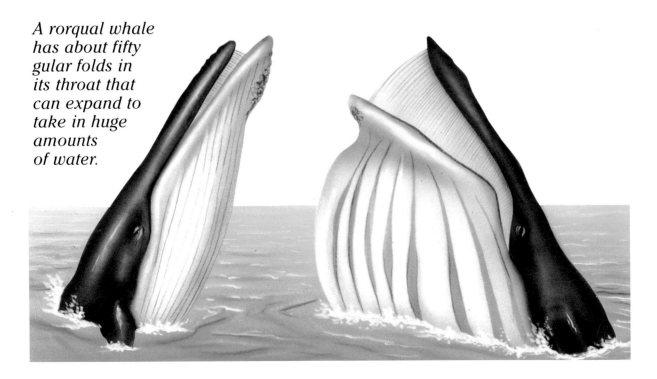

ANCESTORS OF THE WHALES

Primitive cetaceans

Cetaceans spent millions of years evolving under the sea. The first fossil to be discovered was Protocetus, which lived over fifty million years ago. Its body was similar in some ways to today's whales. It had an elongated upper jaw, its eyes were separated, and its teeth were very simple. This creature's primitive hearing apparatus was similar to that of today's whales, which suggests it had already adapted its sense of hearing under water.

Protocetus lived fifty million years ago in the Mediterranean and measured 8 feet (2.5 m) in length.

The teeth of the primitive Mysticetus functioned as a filter.

Mauicetus looked like today's whales but still had to develop baleen.

The first whales

Whales are gigantic creatures with baleen instead of teeth. The evolution from primitive teeth to baleen plates took millions of years. Mauicetus, for example, lived about 24 million years ago in the ocean south of Australia. Its body was not very large, but it had a hydrodynamic shape, well developed fins, and elongated teeth with small protrusions that interconnected when Mauicetus closed its mouth. This formed a type of filter that let water flow out while retaining the captured food.

Did You Know...

that certain whales fish with nets made of bubbles?

When the Pacific humpback whale finds prey, it swims below and starts to circle while letting air escape. The air rises in the form of columns of bubbles that act like a net and trap the fish. The whale moves up through the central column and surfaces with its mouth open, trapping hundreds of pounds of fish at one time.

THE LIFE OF THE GIANTS

Tireless travelers

Whales are experienced travelers. During winter, many rorqual whales travel 5,600 miles (9,000 km) from the Arctic Ocean to the Indian Ocean to mate. Abundant food and a good place to mate are the main reasons for these long migrations. In summer, the krill populations increase in the polar waters, and thousands of whales head there to feed.

The whale's impressive tail is used for mobility and self-defense.

Whales can travel thousands of miles (km) because of their huge energy reserves and light water weight.

SUMMER FEEDING GROUNDS

WINTER REARING GROUNDS

HUMPBACK MIGRATORY ROUTES

The whale's blowhole

Whales surface frequently to breathe air. As they break the water's surface, they eject a column of old air from their lungs at an incredible pressure. This spout is formed by vapor condensation that can be seen and heard from a great distance. The first spout after a deep dive is always the highest, the most powerful, and the one that lasts longest. The shape of the spout varies according to the type and

The whale's blowhole has either one or two holes, or nostrils.

size of the whale, which helps researchers identify the species from far away.

The whale's spout varies in height and shape according to the species.

SPERM WHALE: Up to 16 feet (5 m) in height.

FIN WHALE: From 16 to 26 feet (5 to 8 m) in height.

RIGHT WHALE: 3 to 6.5 feet (1 to 2 m) but can reach 10 feet (3 m).

HUMPBACK WHALE: From 6.5 to 10 feet (2 to 3 m); the first blow can reach 16 feet (5 m).

Expert divers

Whales are expert divers, although their ability depends on the species. The sperm whale dives deepest and stays down longest; it can remain below for over ninety minutes without coming up for air and can reach a depth of over 6,600 feet (2,000 m). Whales hold their breath while diving. For this reason, the whale takes in a lot of oxygen before going under, in that brief moment when it opens its blowhole on the surface to breathe. Whales breathe with less frequency than land mammals, but much deeper to take in more oxygen.

The sperm whale dives head first more than 3,300 feet (1,000 m) in search of giant squid. When it has captured one, the whale rapidly surfaces and kills the squid by the sudden change in pressure.

APPENDIX TO

SECRETS OF THE ANIMAL WORLD

WHALES
Giant Marine Mammals

WHALE SECRETS

In search of a companion.
When the rorqual whale looks for a mate, it swims along the surface of the water while emitting a powerful call that can travel 50 miles (80 km).

▼ High jumps. Sometimes whales like to play by making

enormous leaps, or breaching. They rise entirely out of the water, falling back with a crash. Females and young do the most breaching, especially in large groups of whales.

▼ Moored whales. Scientists believe whales run aground along the coasts because of certain variations in Earth's magnetic field. These variations disorient the animals, which rely on their magnetic sense to guide them.

▼ Scraping the bottom. Gray whales pick up food from the ocean bottom, often leaving characteristic marks there.

▼ Whale products. A giant whale can provide 28 tons (25 metric tons) of oil and almost 2.2 tons (2 metric tons) of baleen plates.

An enormous brain. The blue whale's brain weighs about 15 pounds (7 kg), while an adult human brain weighs 3.3 pounds (1.5 kg).

A great stomach. The whale's stomach is divided into three chambers; the first contains stones, called gastroliths, that are used to break down the enormous amounts of food swallowed by the animal.

1. How much can a whale weigh?
   a) Up to 16.5 tons (15 m. tons).
   b) Up to 55 tons (50 m. tons).
   c) Over 165 tons (150 m. tons).

2. The whale suborder Archaeoceti refers to:
   a) a group of black whales.
   b) a group of extinct whales.
   c) a group of pygmy whales.

3. The largest animal ever to exist on Earth is:
   a) the dinosaur.
   b) the mammoth.
   c) the blue whale.

4. During the lactation period, the calf consumes:
   a) 3.2 gallons (12 l) of milk a day.
   b) 40 gallons (150 l) of milk a day.
   c) 1.3 gallons (5 l) of milk a day.

5. Baleen plates are:
   a) several hairs behind the ears.
   b) several horny plates on the upper jaw.
   c) elongated muscles on tail-fin.

6. Sperm whales feed on:
   a) dolphins.
   b) plankton.
   c) giant squid.

The answers to WHALE SECRETS questions are on page 32.

GLOSSARY

Archaeoceti: an ancient family of whales that is now extinct. The Archaeoceti disappeared from Earth about 45 million years ago.

baleen: flexible whalebone plates in a whale's mouth that act like strainers. These plates scoop tiny organisms from the water for the whale to eat.

blowhole: a hole through which the whale breathes. Whales take in oxygen through the blowhole and spout water vapor from the blowhole.

blubber: the thick fat that keeps a whale warm by trapping heat inside its body. Some whales have blubber up to 2 feet (0.6 m) thick. Blubber stores energy that the whale lives off when food is scarce.

Cetacea: the scientific order to which all whales belong. *Cetacea* is the Latin word for a whale. Cetaceans evolved for millions of years under the sea.

crustaceans: creatures with an exoskeleton, or shell. Lobsters and shrimp are crustaceans. Krill, which resemble small shrimp, are crustaceans. They are also a main source of food for baleen whales.

esophagus: the tube that connects the throat to the stomach. Food must travel down the esophagus to reach the stomach for digestion.

evolve: to change shape or develop gradually over time.

flukes: tail fins that help propel a whale through the water with a wavy, up-and-down motion. Each whale species has a unique fluke, with its own shape and markings.

gestation: the period in the reproduction cycle between conception and birth.

gular folds: grooves on the underside of a rorqual whale. These flexible folds can extend from the mouth of the whale all the way to the navel. The gular folds allow the whale's mouth to greatly expand as it opens.

hydrodynamic: a shape that allows an object to move easily through the water. The whale's hydrodynamic body is smooth and tapered at both ends. This shape helps reduce friction and resistance as the whale moves through the water.

krill: tiny water creatures that resemble shrimp. Krill is a major food source for the baleen whales.

lactation: the process of secreting milk to feed offspring.

migrate: to move from one place or climate to another, usually on a seasonal basis. Baleen whales undertake long migrations to search for food and places to mate.

Mysticeti: baleen whales that have whalebone plates instead of teeth. Humpback, gray, and blue whales belong to the Mysticeti group.

Odontoceti: a group of whales that has teeth. Killer, sperm, and beaked whales belong to this group, as well as dolphins and porpoises.

pectoral fins: the flippers, or arms, of a whale. Pectoral fins extend from the side of the body and help the whale steer its way around in the water.

plankton: tiny plants and animals that drift in the ocean. Plankton is a main food source for baleen whales.

pod: a group of whales.

polar: relating to the regions of Earth that are very cold and icy; specifically, around the North and South poles. Whales migrate to polar regions every year.

prey: animals that are hunted, captured, and killed for food by other animals.

right whales: types of whales that received their name from early whalers who considered them the best whales to hunt because they were slow and yielded good blubber and baleen. The three types of right whales include: the Greenland right whale (also known as the bowhead whale), the pygmy right whale, and the black right whale.

rorquals: certain types of baleen whales, such as the blue, fin, and minke whales, that have grooves running from the mouth to the navel. These grooves allow the whale's mouth to expand when it eats.

taper: to make or become gradually thinner.

temperate: not extreme; relating to climatic zones with warm summers and cold winters that lie between the warm tropics and the cold polar regions.

tropical: relating to the hot, humid regions of Earth near the equator. Tropical areas refer specifically to those regions that lie between the tropic of Cancer (23.5° latitude north of the equator) and the tropic of Capricorn (23.5° latitude south of the equator).

ACTIVITIES

◆ The whaling industry has taken its toll on whale populations, and many species are now endangered. Do some research at the library and find out more about the history of whaling and how earlier cultures depended on whales for their survival. Compare the methods used to hunt whales today with those of the past. Which parts of the whale are valuable today as opposed to the past? Trace the growth of the whaling industry in relation to diminishing whale populations.

◆ Big animals have big meals. Whales eat about 5 percent of their total weight every day — that can be several tons of food! Use a small scale and weigh all the food you eat in one day. Next, find out your own weight. What percent of your body weight were your meals? How much more would you have to eat to consume 5 percent of your body weight?

MORE BOOKS TO READ

Arctic Whales and Whaling. Bobbie Kalman (Crabtree Publishing)
Ibis: A True Whale Story. John Himmelman (Scholastic)
Killer Whales. (Holiday)
Meeting the Whales: The Equinox Guide to Giants of the Deep. (Firefly)
The Sea World Book of Whales. Eve Bunting (Harcourt Brace)
The Search for the Right Whale. Scott Kraus and Ken Mallory (Crown)
The Story of Three Whales. Giles Whittell (Gareth Stevens)
Watching Whales. John F. Waters (Dutton)
The Whale Family Book. Cynthia D'Vincent (Picture Book Studio)
Whale Magic for Kids. Tom Wolpert (Gareth Stevens)
Whales, Dolphins, and Porpoises. Mark Carwardine (Dorling Kindersley)
The Whales: The Sovereigns of the Sea. Brett Caroline (Garrett)
Whaling Days. Carol Carrick (Houghton Mifflin)

VIDEOS

Whale Watcher: The Movie. (Bennett Marine Video)
Whales and Dolphins. (MPI Home Video/ Facets Multimedia)
Whales and the Threat of Nets. (Focus on Animals)
The Whales That Wouldn't Die. (CRM/McGraw-Hill Films)
Whales Weep Not. (Learning Corporation of America/MTI Teleprograms)

PLACES TO VISIT

Kelly Tarlton's Underwater World
23 Tamaki Drive
Auckland
New Zealand

Mystic Marinelife Aquarium
55 Coogan Boulevard
Mystic, CT 06355

Vancouver Aquarium
In Stanley Park
Vancouver, British Columbia
V6B 3X8

John G. Shedd Aquarium
1200 S. Lake Shore Dr.
Chicago, IL 60605

Sea World on the Gold Coast
Sea World Drive Spit
Surfers Paradise
Queensland, Australia 4217

Sea World
1720 South Shores Rd.
San Diego, CA 92109

INDEX

Answers to WHALE SECRETS questions:
1. c
2. b
3. c
4. b
5. b
6. c

CENTRAL ELEMENTARY
SCHOOL